What Christians Should Know About ...

Generational Sin

Pennant Jones

Sovereign World

Unless otherwise indiated all Bible quotations are taken from
the HOLY BIBLE, New International Version.
Copyright © 1973, 1978, 1984 by International Bible Society.
Used by Permission.

ISBN: 1 85240 259 8

This Sovereign World book is distributed in North America by
Renew Books, a ministry of Gospel Light, Ventura, California, USA.
For a free catalog of resources from Renew Books/Gospel Light,
please contact your Christian supplier or call 1-800-4-GOSPEL.

SOVEREIGN WORLD LIMITED
P.O. Box 777, Tonbridge, Kent TN11 0ZS, England.

Typeset and printed in the UK by Sussex Litho Ltd, Chichester, West Sussex.

Contents

4

Foreword

When speaking about generational sin, I have often shown photographs of my son and myself, both of them taken when we were about eighteen months old. They are remarkably similar and usually most people think that my son's photo is me! We do indeed inherit many characteristics from our parents, whether we like it or not. It is not difficult to think of well-known footballers, cricketers and other athletes, who have parents who have also been good sportsmen or women, often in the same sport. The same is true of many musicians, doctors, engineers, actors and other artists who have clearly inherited talents and abilities that run in their family. This inheritance comes mainly through the genes passed on to us from our parents and ancestors, but we also learn from our parents and unconsciously copy them in the ways we act and speak. How many teenage daughters have been embarrassed, like my sister was, when boyfriends have launched into a conversation on the telephone, only to be interrupted by "Excuse me, this is her mother speaking!"? My cousin tells me that I have a mannerism that reminds her of my father, but she will not tell me what it is, in case I should become self-conscious about it and stop doing what for her is a reminder of an uncle she loved. Now she tells me that my son has a chuckle just like me!

However, to attribute all that we inherit just to genes and learned behaviour is not the full story. There is also a spiritual aspect of inheritance that passes down our generational line. In this book I seek to explain what the Bible teaches about our inheritance and how any negative effects on us of sins in past generations can be recognised and dealt with through the work of Christ on the cross.

There have been many occasions when my wife, Maureen, and

I have been privileged to pray with people about the way they have been affected by the sins of others and especially of their ancestors. During the time we were leaders at the Ellel Ministries centre at Glyndley Manor in East Sussex we saw many who received healing in their bodies, in their damaged emotions and wills, and in other ways. We saw marriages saved and many people set free to make right relationships in a way they had never been able to before. The prayer steps outlined in this book for dealing with family background and inheritance, were frequently the first key to this healing and freedom. The principles are truly liberating. They are part of what Jesus did when He came to set captives free. Some short accounts of ways in which people have been helped have been included. There is of course much more to each story and the names have been changed to protect the identities of the people concerned. Maureen has helped, encouraged and advised me in the writing of this book and I record my thanks to her for this. We are both grateful to our friend Dr Harold Dewberry of Rancho Cucamonga, California. It was through his biblical teaching that we first grasped the full significance of this important yet neglected subject.

1

What is
generational sin?

Bill was a delivery man who had to walk daily in his job. As each day wore on, one leg became more and more painful and he had to take painkillers just to finish the day's work. After months of pain, tests eventually revealed that he had a tiny hair-line fracture in his shin. There was no medical reason why it should not heal normally and Bill was told to be patient and it would heal. But it didn't and the pain went on for two years. Bill had other problems in his life too, emotional pain from things in the past, and he came seeking help over these. In talking to him, it emerged that Bill's father had been deeply into freemasonry, but Bill had refused to have anything to do with it.

Soon it became clear that the masonic rituals and oaths taken by his father were somehow seriously affecting areas of Bill's life. His release from these effects started as he was led through prayers like those outlined in this book. His emotional pain began to be healed and he returned home. He telephoned a few days later to tell us that his leg pain had lessened day by day and was now completely gone. He knew the healing process had taken place. Although there had been no specific prayer for his leg pain, once the effects of sins of earlier generations had been dealt with, a barrier which had clearly inhibited natural healing was removed.

Julia had waited for prayer after a meeting and shared with us that she had feelings that she had been abused sexually by her father. She acknowledged that she had no actual recollection of this and found it hard to believe that he would have done such a thing. Yet her feelings were real and were badly affecting her life. She told us that she had always found it difficult to make relationships especially with men. Although Julia knew her father really cared for her, she had always felt some barrier between them. As my wife and I talked with her, we wondered if the root of her problem could be in the sin of a past generation. "Yes" she said, "I do remember hearing that one of my father's grandparents had been immoral sexually in some way, but I have no idea what it was."

We led her in prayers similar to those shown later in the book. As we began I laid my hand gently on her shoulder, but she recoiled sharply, saying "Don't touch me, I can't bear a man touching me." As we prayed, Julia took hold of the truth that on the cross Jesus had borne the iniquities of earlier generations which affected her. She wept as the emotional pain of years was lifted. Julia was wonderfully set free. It was as if she had been released from prison. When it was finished she gave me a big hug; something she could never have done previously. It was clear that the root of Julia's problems lay in some sin of earlier generations in her family and was nothing to do with her father. Dealing with that generational iniquity was the key to her liberty, enabling her to build normal relationships that had been impossible before.

What the Bible says

> *You shall not make for yourself an idol in the form of anything in heaven above or on the earth beneath or in the waters below. You shall not bow down to them or worship them; for I, the Lord your God, am a jealous God, punishing the children for the sin of the fathers to the third and fourth generation of those who hate me, but showing love to a thousand generations of those who love me and keep my commandments.* (Exodus 20:4-6)

In this text from the ten commandments God makes it clear that idolatry has consequences that will affect children to the third and fourth generation. We cannot avoid this scripture. The ten commandments are God's law for all people and all time. There are also similar passages in Exodus 34, Deuteronomy 5 and Numbers 14, where the principle clearly applies to all sin, not just idolatry.

The Lord is slow to anger, abounding in love and forgiving sin and rebellion. Yet he does not leave the guilty unpunished; he punishes the children for the sin of the fathers to the third and fourth generation. (Numbers 14:18)

It is significant that these passages all include a declaration of God's compassion and mercy. There is clearly no limit to the flow of mercy and blessing down the generations. We still have a long way to go before we get to a thousand generations from the time when Moses received the ten commandments! The fact that children do suffer consequences from their parents' sins should not be viewed as the act of an unfair God. All sin has bad results. The principle of reaping the consequences of what we sow is clear in scripture. The effect of one generation's sin on another is a particular application of this principle of sowing and reaping.

Do not be deceived: God cannot be mocked. A man reaps what he sows. (Galatians 6:7)

Sow for yourselves righteousness, reap the fruit of unfailing love... But you have planted wickedness, you have reaped evil ... (Hosea 10:12-13)

It is not that God is vindictive in punishing children for the sins of their parents; it is merely an acknowledgement of the fact that all sin brings bad consequences. Such consequences fall not only upon the sinner but also on their descendants. Our experiences of everyday life, and the sad stories we often read in newspapers show only too well that children do suffer because their parents sin. There are many examples of this in scripture too. Nevertheless we should take heart from these Bible passages that declare that God is slow to anger and abounds in love. God clearly intends that love and mercy should flow unhindered from generation to generation. This love and mercy culminated in the finished work of Christ on the cross which dealt with every aspect of sin including the effects of generational sin.

From everlasting to everlasting the Lord's love is with those who fear him, and his righteousness with their children's children, with those who keep his covenant and remember to obey his precepts. (Psalm 103:17-18)

In Deuteronomy there is a reference to the consequences of the disobedience of entering into a marriage forbidden by God.

No one born of a forbidden marriage nor any of his descendants may enter the assembly of the Lord, even down to the tenth generation. (Deuteronomy. 23:2)

This implies that this particular disobedience of entering into a sexual relationship outside what God allowed had spiritual consequences that would have defiled the sanctuary for as long as ten generations. This indicates that sexual sins may have a long term effect. In general, however, it seems that God in His mercy limits the effects of ancestral sin to three or four generations, while there is no limit to the flow of blessing and mercy down the family line.

How are we affected by our parents' sins?

First of all we cannot escape the fact that the whole human race is subject to the consequences of the fall of Adam.

Sin entered the world through one man, and death through sin, and in this way death came to all men, because all sinned. (Romans 5:12)

So as part of the human race, we are "in Adam" and are all subject to death and separation from God. Our own sin perpetuates that separation until we accept and appropriate the truth that we can be made alive in Christ.

For since death came through a man, the resurrection of the dead comes also through a man. For as in Adam all die, so in Christ all will be made alive. (1 Corinthians 16:21-22)

10

The wages of sin is death, but the gift of God is eternal life in Christ Jesus our Lord. (Romans 6:23)

God warned His people that problems affecting following generations would arise if they were disobedient to His laws. For example in Leviticus 26 God spelled out the blessings that would flow if His people were careful to obey His commands, and the disasters that would follow disobedience.

Those who are left will waste away in the lands of their enemies because of their sins; also because of their fathers' sins they will waste away. But if they will confess their sins and the sins of their fathers... then when their hearts are humbled... I will remember my covenant with Jacob and my covenant with Isaac and my covenant with Abraham, and I will remember the land. (Leviticus 26:39-42)

Here is the offer of hope that confession from a humble heart will open the way to God's love and mercy.

The Bible uses several words to describe different categories of sin. **Sin** means falling short, error, failure, missing the mark. **Transgression** is the deliberate breaking of laws and rules laid down by God. **Trespass** is going into territory or behaviour that God forbids. **Disobedience** is knowing what should be done and failing to do it, or doing what is known to be wrong in the sight of God. **Rebellion** is refusing to accept God's authority. **Iniquity** is the lawless nature, the tendency to sin that we inherit from Adam and our ancestors. It is defined in dictionaries as gross injustice, misfortune, lawlessness and perverseness. It is used in the Bible to express the acts of the wicked against the righteous. One of its applications is the unfairness of sin, for example when we sin against others and they suffer, or others sin against us and we suffer. The word iniquity is thus a good one to use for the sins of previous generations that affect us and that inherited tendency to sin that is part of our nature. Modern versions of the Bible frequently translate the word as **wickedness**. The same words translated as iniquity are also given the meanings of vanity, mischief, perverseness, wrong and misery.

11

In the sermon on the mount (Matthew 5:21-30), Jesus showed how sins we may commit can begin with iniquity in the heart. He quoted the law saying that anyone who committed murder would be judged and went on to say "But I tell you that anyone who is angry with his brother will be subject to judgment." Similarly in the case of adultery he said, "Anyone who looks at a woman lustfully has already committed adultery with her in his heart." The sins are murder and adultery but the root of these is the iniquity of hatred and lust that is in the heart by nature.

When we suffer consequences from our ancestors' sins, we experience the unfairness and the injustice of their iniquity. But this same iniquity becomes part of our own make up. There can be weaknesses and compulsions in us as a result of our forebears' sins. Traumatic events and deeply emotional experiences such as grief in our parents, or even our grandparents, can affect us too. It is remarkable how a similar pattern of behaviour can appear in generation after generation of the same family. For example alcoholism frequently recurs in families, even when rising generations have vowed to avoid it and become teetotal after experiencing its devastating effects in their childhood. When the results of a survey on divorce were published, one newspaper ran the headline "Divorce is hereditary." The statistics showed that a high proportion of divorcees were themselves from broken families. Sadly, abuse of children whether violent, verbal, emotional or sexual is also frequently repeated in one generation after another. Often an abuser will admit to having been abused as a child. Nevertheless the fact that such things do recur in families by no means makes them inevitable and we should never assume that they will automatically happen.

One of the most damaging ways parents can harm their children is by what they say. Statements made by parents or other family members, especially if they are frequently repeated, can act as a curse on a child even if this was never intended to be so. Typical examples of the kind of statement made are: "No son of mine is seen crying." "Nobody in our family is practical with their hands." " Learning music or art is a waste of time." "Women in this family are independent, they don't need men." "All our eldest sons follow their father's footsteps (in the business, as a doctor, in the services, as a clergyman etc.)." "Children in our family must keep up its high academic standards." "Men in this family die young." "Our family can never save money." Some of the statements may well be accurate descriptions of the family, but when repeated frequently they begin to bind the rising generation in a family in an unhelpful, restricting and unnecessary way. Sometimes a parent who has failed to fulfil dreams tries to express them through a child. Great pressure may be put on the child to achieve in areas where they have no natural ability, while stifling potential where they do. Career choice has sometimes been forced on people causing much damage. Children may, of course, freely choose to follow the same paths as their parents or paths that greatly please them. When this is the case no damage will be done.

The Bible recognises the power of the tongue and its destructive capability. James describes the tongue *as a fire, a world of iniquity* that corrupts the whole person. He goes on to say that with the tongue *we bless our God and Father, and with it we curse men. Out of the same mouth proceed blessing and cursing.* (James 3:6-10 AV) There is much about the power of the tongue in the Proverbs.

> *The tongue that brings healing is a tree of life, but a deceitful tongue crushes the spirit.*   (Proverbs 15:4)

> *The tongue has the power of life and death.* (Proverbs 18:21)

The Bible also contains examples of sins and weaknesses continuing through several generations. The tendency of one king after another to fall into idolatry is recorded with monotonous regularity in the history of Judah and Israel with words like: *He did evil in the eyes of the Lord, as his fathers had done.*

Even in the lives of the Patriarchs there was a repeated misuse of their wives in one way or another. Abraham abused his wife by using her to protect himself when he lied describing Sarah as his sister. (Genesis 12:10-20) Isaac did the same (Genesis 26:7) and also misused Rebekah when he sought to be mothered by her instead of treating her properly as a wife. (Genesis 24:67) She lost all respect for him and plotted with her favourite son Jacob to trick Isaac. In his turn Jacob was tricked into marrying Leah, but though he never loved her, he had sexual relations with her. She bore him four sons and the names she gave them reveal the pain in her heart as she sought but never found her husband's love. (Genesis 29:31-35).

When David cried out to God for mercy after his adultery with Bathsheba, he acknowledged that there was iniquity in his family background.

> *Have mercy upon me, O God, according to your loving-kindness. ...Wash me thoroughly from my iniquity and cleanse me from my sin. ...I was brought forth in iniquity and in sin my mother conceived me.* (Psalm 51:1-5 NKJV)

Whose fault is it then?

It is all too easy to say, "It's not my fault. It's in my genes. I can't help it. It's the way I am. This is the way my family is." Our genes do indeed determine much of our nature and abilities. Genetic weaknesses can make some people more vulnerable towards some illnesses. Conditions and illnesses, like haemophilia and cystic fibrosis, for example, only occur because they are passed on in genes. In general though, a genetic predisposition does not have to mean that a particular illness is inevitable. Similarly a history of particular sin in our family background may make us vulnerable in the same area. In spite of our genetic make up and the fact that we all have a tendency to sin, and possibly to sin in exactly the same way as our parents, we cannot be absolved from responsibility. The Bible makes it very clear that we are all responsible for our own behaviour.

> *The soul who sins is the one who will die. The son will not share the guilt of the father, nor will the father share the guilt of the son.* (Ezekiel 18:20)

This text shows that it is those who commit sin who are guilty before God. Our eternal life is not affected by our ancestors' sins and iniquities, though we may suffer from their consequences. We are not personally guilty of those sins so they will not affect our salvation. However, if we sin in a way which affects our children, then we are clearly responsible and God will judge us accordingly.

> *In those days people will no longer say, 'The fathers have eaten sour grapes, and the children's teeth are set on edge.' Instead, everyone will die for his own sin.*
>
> (Jeremiah 31:29-30)

This passage from Jeremiah comes in the context of a prophecy of the new covenant that God was going to establish. It points ahead to the Lord Jesus Christ and to His work on the cross that would save people from their sins and also liberate them from the effects of generational iniquity.

2

How God deals with generational iniquity

We have looked at the bad news of how we inherit the effects of generational iniquity and have iniquity in our hearts by nature, but there is good news too. First let us be grateful that blessings pass unhindered down the generational line. It is all too easy to concentrate on the evil and suffering we may experience, so it is always right to pause to count our blessings and thank God for everything good in our inheritance. The greatest good news is that when Jesus suffered and died on the cross He not only dealt with our own sins; He dealt with the effects of generational iniquity too. We need to take hold of both of these truths for ourselves in order to receive their beneficial effect.

When John the Baptist saw Jesus at the River Jordan he said, *"Look, the Lamb of God, who takes away the sin of the world!"* Those who heard Jesus described in this way would immediately think of the sacrifices required by the laws of Moses, especially of the Passover Lamb. A study of the sacrifices described in the Old Testament, like the Passover, helps us to understand the seriousness of sin and to appreciate the full meaning of Jesus' death on the cross.

Another Old Testament ritual points to the way in which Jesus would deal with generational iniquity as well as personal sin. This is the Day of Atonement which was one of the most important events in the Israelite calendar. Leviticus 16 describes how on that day Aaron the High Priest was to take two male goats from the Israelite community:

> *Then he is to take the two goats and present them before the Lord at the entrance to the Tent of Meeting. He is to cast lots for the two goats – one lot for the Lord and the other for the*

17

scapegoat. Aaron shall bring the goat whose lot falls to the Lord and sacrifice it for a sin offering. But the goat chosen by lot as the scapegoat shall be presented alive before the Lord to be used for making atonement by sending it into the desert as a scapegoat.   (Leviticus 16:7-10)

The sacrificed goat was an offering for the people's own sins. Just like the Passover Lamb, the death of this goat was a symbol foreshadowing what one day Jesus would do when He died for the sins of the world. The consequence of our sin is death, but the Gospel Good News is that Jesus' blood was shed for us so that all who believe may live.

You were redeemed ... with the precious blood of Christ, a lamb without blemish or defect.   (1Peter 1:18-19)

The instructions for the scapegoat on the Day of Atonement followed.

He (Aaron) is to lay both hands on the head of the live goat and confess over it all the iniquities of the children of Israel, and all their transgressions, concerning all their sins, putting them on the head of the goat and shall send it away into the wilderness by the hand of a suitable man. The goat shall bear on itself all their iniquities to an uninhabited land; and he shall release the goat in the wilderness.
                    (Leviticus 16:21-22 NKJV)

The life of the sacrificed goat was given as an offering of blood for cleansing from sin, but the scapegoat did not die. Its life was retained but it was burdened with the iniquities of the nation as a whole and led out of the city to bear them away, thus separating the people from these iniquities.

Isaiah 53 is a wonderful prophecy of the passion of our Lord Jesus and it includes a description of how He would carry our iniquities in His bruised and pierced body at the cross.

He was pierced for our transgressions, he was crushed for

18

our iniquities; the punishment that brought us peace was upon him, and by his wounds we are healed. We all, like sheep, have gone astray, each of us has turned to his own way; and the Lord has laid on him the iniquity of us all.

(Isaiah 53:5-6)

My righteous Servant shall justify many, for he shall bear their iniquities. (Isaiah 53:11)

His blood was shed for the sins of the whole world, but each of us has to come to that place where we realise that "He did it for me." We take hold of this truth individually and in believing it we are born again and receive the gift of new life in Him. But there is more to the Cross than the shed blood of our Lord Jesus. Before He died, his body was bruised and punished for our iniquities. He was beaten and scourged and, like the scapegoat, was led outside the city. There He died as the Lamb of God and took the death penalty for sin in our place, but when the iniquity of us all was laid on His bruised body, Jesus was also our scapegoat. Here He dealt with that category of sin that affects us all, the iniquity we inherit, the effects of other people's sins on us. It is a category of sin that, although we suffer its consequences, does not require blood sacrifice in place of our death, because it is not our sin, but the result of others' sins.

When Jesus instituted the Lord's Supper, He said "This is my body which is broken for you, and this is my blood of the New Covenant, which is shed for you." How thankful we should be that not only was His blood shed for us, but that His body was bruised for us too. He is the Lamb of God, but He is also the scapegoat when He bears away the iniquity of us all. How wonderful it is that when we take the cup we can remember that His blood was shed for us, for our sins, and when we take the broken bread we remember that His body was bruised when He bore our iniquity.

Just as when we take hold of the truth that Jesus died for our sins, we are born again, so also we need to take hold of the truth that Jesus carried for us the iniquities of our ancestors and of others whose sins may have affected us. Taking hold of this truth and applying it in our lives can be wonderfully liberating and healing.

3

How to apply
this truth

We need to do several things when we apply this truth about
generational iniquity for ourselves or when we pray with other
people. First we need to confess and acknowledge the sins of our
ancestors, as God has commanded. Then it is good to recognise
our position as a family member and personally to turn from the
sins and weaknesses that have been acknowledged. We should
humble ourselves by examining our own lives asking questions
like: "Have I sinned in the same way?", "Do I need to repent of
these same things in my own life?", "Have I reacted in an ungodly
way to those who sinned against me?" We will then need to pray
prayers of repentance in response to such questions, asking for
cleansing by the blood of Jesus. We should go on to express our
forgiveness to those who have sinned against us, including our
parents, and other ancestors. We must recognise that one effect of
previous generations' sins on us is the building of ungodly bonds
between us and our forebears. Where such a wrong bond exists
we shall need to pray for it to be broken. This can lead into prayer
for physical healing or healing of damaged emotions and if
necessary for deliverance and freedom from any foothold Satan
may have established through the family line. Finally we should
pray for a renewal of the mind and for an infilling with the Holy
Spirit. The following paragraphs explain these steps.

Confession and Repentance

On the Day of Atonement the High Priest was required to lay his
hands on the head of the scapegoat and confess over it all the
iniquities of the Israelites. These were the sins of the whole

people, of the nation and families into which they had been born. In the same way we can confess the sins and iniquities of our forebears that may have affected us. In confession, we are not telling God something He does not know about iniquity in the family line and we are not declaring to God that we are in any way responsible for other people's sins. Confession is simply speaking out the facts as far as we know them. In confessing the sins of our ancestors we agree with God that they are, or were, sinners in ways that may or may not be known to us and that these sins will have affected us. We cannot repent on behalf of our ancestors; they are responsible for their own actions before God. Nevertheless we are part of the same family and can choose to turn away from all such sins and weaknesses. Where we have similar sins of our own, we shall need to confess them too, and ask for cleansing by the blood of Jesus.

The Bible contains several accounts of people confessing the sins of their fathers in accordance with God's instructions. When he heard of the destruction of Jerusalem, Nehemiah wept, fasted and prayed over the sad news he had received. He recognised that its root cause was the sin in previous generations who had not been obedient to God's commands. He identified himself with them. His prayer was one of confession and simply begged for God's mercy on the present generation if they returned to Him in obedience:

> *Oh Lord, ...let your ear be attentive and your eyes open to hear the prayer your servant is praying before you day and night for your servants, the people of Israel. I confess the sins we Israelites, including myself and my father's house, have committed against you.* (Nehemiah 1:6)

Later all the people followed Nehemiah's example and confessed their fathers' sins in great detail.

> *Our forefathers, became arrogant and stiff-necked, and did not obey your commands. They refused to listen and failed to remember the miracles you performed among them. They became stiff-necked and in their rebellion appointed a leader*

22

in order to return to their slavery. But you are a forgiving God, gracious and compassionate, slow to anger and abounding in love. Therefore you did not desert them.

(Nehemiah 9:16-17)

Daniel also pleaded with God with a heart full of sorrow and repentance. He prayed that God would have mercy and bring the captivity in Babylon to an end. Daniel's prayer too was one of confession when he prayed:

We have sinned and committed iniquity, we have done wickedly and rebelled; even by departing from Your precepts and Your judgements. Neither have we heeded Your servants the prophets, who spoke in Your name to our kings and our princes, to our fathers, and all the people of the land.
Our sins and the iniquities of our fathers have made Jerusalem and your people an object of scorn to all those around us.
Give ear, O God, and hear; open your eyes and see the desolation of the city that bears your Name. We do not make requests of you because we are righteous, but because of your great mercy.
O Lord, listen! O Lord, forgive!   (Daniel 9:5-6,16,18-19)

The Song of the Three Holy Children in the Apocrypha tells us the words of a song that Shadrach, Meshach and Abednego sang when they were cast into the fiery furnace. (Daniel 3)

They walked in the midst of the fire, praising God, and blessing the Lord. ...and prayed, ...O Lord God of our fathers: thy name is worthy to be praised and glorified for evermore, for thou art righteous in all the things that thou hast done to us: yea true are all thy works, thy ways are right and all thy judgements truth. In all the things that thou hast brought upon us, and upon the holy city of our fathers, even Jerusalem, thou hast executed true judgement; for according to truth and judgement didst thou bring all these things upon us because of our sins, for we have sinned and

23

committed iniquity, departing from thee.   (Verses 3 – 6 AV)

Nehemiah, Daniel, and his three friends were all righteous men, but in spite of what was happening to them, they identified themselves with the sins of their ancestors and acknowledged that God was not being unfair to them. They knew that what they were suffering was the consequence of sins in previous generations and their prayers of confession acknowledged this. They acted on God's promise that if they confessed their sins and the sins of their fathers and humbled their hearts, He would remember His covenant with Israel.

Forgiveness

To be released from the effects of our forebears' iniquity we must not only acknowledge and confess their sin, but go on to forgive them for their sins which have affected us. This does not mean that God will forgive them in answer to our prayer, but that we choose to forgive them ourselves. In doing this we take full responsibility for our own lives and stop looking over our generational shoulders for reasons why things have gone wrong in our lives. We might like to pray that our ancestors still living may come to see the full salvation there is in Christ and ask for forgiveness themselves. We need to forgive them in obedience to the instruction Jesus gave us for prayer when He taught His disciples how to pray. It is significant that after teaching them the model "Lord's Prayer", Jesus added this comment on one of its petitions:

> *For if you forgive men when they sin against you, your heavenly Father will also forgive you. But if you do not forgive men their sins, your Father will not forgive your sins.*
> (Matthew 6:14-15)

We therefore need to forgive those who have sinned against us in obedience to Jesus' teaching here and in other places in the Gospels. It may be very difficult to do this, especially for those who have experienced severe abuse or neglect from parents. If we remain unforgiving, we are actually holding ourselves in a bondage. It is as though we are linked by an unseen chain to the person we need to forgive and about whom we have negative emotions and feelings. Forgiveness is a choice; it is an act of the will. When we choose to forgive we begin to release ourselves from the restraining bonds of unforgiveness. We may not feel like forgiving. The emotional pain of past hurts may still be very real. But if we are to be free and able to receive healing and forgiveness ourselves, it is essential that we make the choice to forgive. We can do it as an act of our will in a simple prayer to God.

When we choose to forgive those whose sin has affected us, we are not saying that it does not matter. It does indeed matter, and those who sinned will be accountable for their sins before God. After we have made the choice to forgive, it is not necessary to tell the person that we have forgiven them. Indeed it may well be that many of those concerned are no longer alive, especially if they are from more than one generation before us. If those we have forgiven are still very much part of our life, we do not have to renew a trusting relationship with them straight away, as if nothing had ever happened to hurt us. Doing this very thing has often merely given an opportunity for further damage. Fractured trust needs time to be restored and in some situations may never be restored. The fact that we have forgiven does not mean that we have to remain in an abusive situation.

Following God's way brings a freedom which is like removing blinkers so that we can see the wider scene and make better choices for the future. Where there is forgiveness, relationships may sometimes change because the person who has been forgiven will also be spiritually released from our part of the bonding and their behaviour may change as a result. If this happens, relationships might be renewed and restored. But even if this is not possible, forgiveness is God's way and we must follow it.

Paul said that he wanted to press on to take hold of all that there is in Christ (Philippians 3:12) and encouraged us to do the same. If we go on holding on to others in unforgiveness, waiting to get our own back sometime, then it is very difficult for us to take hold of Christ. Added to this our heart will grow hard and bitter.

Jesus taught us that forgiveness should be a way of life for a Christian. When He said we should forgive seventy-times-seven He meant that it should be a continual attitude. Experience has shown that forgiveness often needs to be repeated several times towards the same person and even for the same sin. At first, forgiving is an act of the will, a choice, but as we go on doing it, our emotions become involved too as it comes from deeper and deeper within us. As damaged emotions are healed this becomes easier. It may of course be that the same offences are repeated again and again against us and we shall need the overflowing love of Jesus in our hearts to go on offering the gift of forgiveness repeatedly.

Jesus Himself gave us the supreme example when He was being nailed to the cross. At the very moment His body was being pierced, His cry was "Father forgive them, they know not what they do."

4

Understanding
Soul-ties

Good and Bad Ties

We all have relationships and ties with other people. Often the term soul-tie is used to describe such bonds when they hold us in close and enduring relationships. Good relationships among family and friends are what give meaning to life and are very important for our well-being. The first and most important soul-ties we make are with our parents. They begin in the womb and become strong and enduring through childhood. As we grow up we begin to establish soul-ties with others, brothers and sisters, aunts and uncles, grandparents, friends, colleagues at work and so on. Some of these relationships may be superficial but where they are deep, an enduring tie will be formed.

Friendship ties, like the one between David and Jonathan, (1 Samuel 20:17) can be especially rewarding and bring much pleasure and satisfaction. For those who marry, the bond between husband and wife becomes the most important human relationship in life. Such ties are good; they enrich life and bring much blessing. In his letters, Paul often prayed that the members of the churches he was writing to would develop good ties between them. For example to the church at Philippi he wrote:

> *Fulfill my joy by being like-minded, having the same love,*
> *being of one accord, of one mind.*   (Philippians 2:2)

The Greek word he uses for "one accord" is *sumpsuchoi* which literally means alike-in-soul. Clearly Paul wanted good soul-ties to be established between members of the same church fellowship. Later in the same chapter Paul describes his relationship with Timothy as *isopsuchon* or identical-in-soul. His relationship with Timothy was, as he said, as a son with his father. He was saying to the Philippians that when they met Timothy it was as if they would be meeting Paul himself, they were so close and so alike. Jesus wants His disciples to be bonded together in love and care for each other.

As I have loved you, so you must love one another.
(John 13:34)

It is a fact that we do become like those to whom we are closely tied. Husbands and wives who have lived together for years tend to become more and more like each other. This should not be a restricting tie but a relationship of love and trust where each is known to the other and where there is freedom bounded by care for one another. Those who work in the same place tend to adopt the "culture" of the organisation. In fact many organisations try to increase employee loyalty and bonding by offering opportunities for social activities linked to the business or other benefits like share option schemes.

Knowing that we grow to be like those to whom we are tied, Paul prayed that we should have a close relationship with our Lord Jesus and so become like Him. He spoke of us being *"conformed to the image of His Son"* and of *"being transformed into His likeness with ever-increasing glory"*. (Romans 8:29, 2 Corinthians 3:18) The bonding we have as Christians with Jesus and through Him with our Heavenly Father is the most important relationship a human being can enjoy. It should be a model for our other relationships. In all of them, we should in humility consider others better than ourselves and have the same attitude as Christ. (Philippians 2:5-11)

Soul-ties, then, can and should be good and a blessing to us, but sadly not all ties are good. Some ties that began in a good way can turn sour. For example, babies are totally dependent on their parents, especially the mother. However, the aim should be that over the years, as the child grows up, he or she should be being continuously prepared for independence. Sometimes from within good bonding with a loving and caring parent, an ungodly strand can grow and develop. Where children are so controlled that they cannot make their own decisions as they grow up into adulthood, an ungodly soul-tie of domination comes into being. This tie can restrict a person long into their adult life, continuing even after the parent has died. Children who are abused emotionally, physically or sexually also have ungodly ties with those who have abused them. These are particularly strong where family members are concerned. Strong ungodly ties are also formed through hatred, jealousy or fear which are powerful emotions. Within the family, soul-ties will often be partly good and partly bad, leading to much confusion.

Ungodly ties can also grow though experiences of grief or disappointment. Where grief has grown and overwhelmed us without being dissipated and healed over a natural period of time, a bond with one who has died can be perpetuated in a way not intended by God. The effects of war or trauma in the family background are sometimes very strong and can be the root of abnormal grief and anxiety in families. Where this is the case, the grief and pain of previous generations can be acknowledged. We can ask God to break the ungodly part of the tie, since He does not want us to be burdened in this way. As we recognise that Jesus bore our iniquity and carried our sorrows we can let the pain and grief of the generations go and be comforted.

We must also be aware that ungodly ties can be formed through our own sin against others. If our sin damages our own children then the generational effects will continue.

Marriage Ties

Wrong ties with parents can affect a marriage. For example, domination or possessiveness by parents can affect the choices of the couple. Rejection by father or mother may have sown a seed which deep down expects rejection from the one close to us and interprets words, actions or attitudes of the spouse as rejection which was never intended. The sexual part of marriage was planned by God to increase and deepen godly bonding, as well as for procreation. When he wrote to the

Corinthians (1 Corinthians 6:15-20) Paul showed how a sexual union creates a lasting bond, involving the soul and spirit as well as the body, whenever it takes place. Sexual relationships outside marriage form ungodly soul-ties which can bring cursing rather than blessing on the people involved and on future generations. If one or both partners in a marriage had sexual encounters before marriage, it is as though these other sexual partners are brought into the marriage. Confession and repentance with prayer to break these ungodly ties will be needed. Writing to the church in Corinth, where sexual immorality was common, Paul said: *I am jealous for you with a godly jealousy. I promised you to one husband, to Christ, so that I might present you as a pure virgin to him.* (1 Corinthians 11:2). This is a picture of how God intended man and woman to come together in marriage. Praise God that Jesus is able to save to the uttermost and that we can be set free and cleansed from the effects of such wrong relationships whether they are our own or were in a previous generation.

We have seen how good soul-ties can be a blessing by making us like those with whom we are bonded. Unfortunately the principle still applies when a tie is ungodly and unhelpful traits can be transferred. It is this that makes those who have been abused often turn into abusers themselves. Those hurt by alcoholism or divorce in their family, even when they do not want to follow those paths, can fall into the same pattern because ungodly soul-ties exist. Where there are ungodly ties, illnesses, calamities and tragedies that happen in families can have deep effects on succeeding generations making them vulnerable to the same sicknesses and liable to suffer abnormal levels of emotions like grief and anger.

Generational iniquity and ungodly soul-ties offer Satan an access route from previous generations into our lives which he is all too ready to exploit. This is particularly so when there has been occult involvement in the family. By dealing with iniquities and ungodly ties in God's way, we can close the door against demonic power and weaken Satan's influence in our lives.

So it is good news that because Jesus has borne the iniquity in His bruised and broken body on the cross, we can be released from the effects of such ungodly ties. Jesus also carried our griefs and bore our sorrows, so we can also be healed from the effects of grief, sorrow and disappointment in the family background and in our own lives. After we have confessed the iniquity, turned from that sin ourselves and forgiven those whose sins have affected us, we can pray that ungodly soul-ties will be broken. In doing this, we are in effect applying the truth of what Jesus did on the cross to our own situation. It is as though we are placing the cross between us and those with whom the ungodly tie exists. We can say "The cross is now between us. Jesus bore the iniquity for me. It stops at the cross. The ungodly soul-tie is broken!"

5

Helping
others

*Confess your sins to each other and pray for each other so
that you may be healed. The prayer of a righteous man is
powerful and effective.* (James 5:16)

It is helpful for Christians to pray with one another when
dealing with generational sin and other negative effects in the
family background. It is helpful to be witnesses to each other's
prayers. Remember that Jesus said *"Where two or three come
together in my name, there am I with them"* (Matthew 18:20).

In the last part of this book, guidance is given on how to apply
the principles described and how to pray with others. Some
example prayer outlines are included.

Family Trees

When praying with others about generational iniquity, it is often
helpful to sketch out a family tree of the person. A chart like the
one in Figure 1 can be used for this purpose.

Ask the person you are praying for to put their own name in the
box at the bottom centre. Then together complete the chart as far as
can be done. Write in the names of brothers, sisters, parents, aunts,
uncles grandparents etc. When as many names as possible are
entered, begin talking about what the person's parents were like.
Ask about their relationships, significant events in their parents'
lives and so on. Position in the family could be important, for
example, eldest or youngest, only child or one of a large family.
Write details on the chart and slowly a picture of the family will
emerge. We have found that very few people know much about

OUTLINE FOR A FAMILY TREE

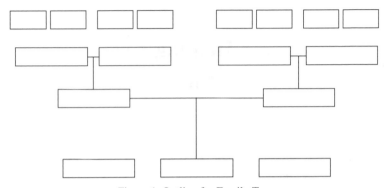

Figure 1 Outline for Family Tree

their great-grandparents, but write in even sketchy information. For example, one coming from another nation or culture may give a clue to some family traits. Adapt the family tree diagram as necessary. For example, if a child's mother died and they were brought up by an aunt or grandmother, emphasise this on the tree. Add into the chart relevant details about the person him/herself by writing them under the box at the bottom. A completed chart will nearly always reveal patterns, events, examples of sinful behaviour and weaknesses in the family background and point to ungodly soul-ties which will need to be dealt with. If the person was adopted, hardly any details of the natural family may be known, but there will always have been some rejection whatever the reason for the adoption; death of a parent, poverty or sexual sin. Remember that you can pray confessing the sins of ancestors even when you are unaware of what they are (Leviticus 5:17-18).

As you pray with another person ask God to send the Holy Spirit to guide you. You may be surprised at what comes to mind and what God shows you, but be sure it is fact and not just imagination.

Parents

Listen, my sons, to a father's instruction; pay attention and

34

gain understanding. I give you sound learning, so do not forsake my teaching. When I was a boy in my father's house, still tender, and an only child of my mother, he taught me and said, "Lay hold of my words with all your heart; keep my commands and you will live." (Proverbs 4:1-4)

What our fathers have told us, we will not hide from our children; we will tell the next generation the praiseworthy deeds of the Lord, his power, and the wonders he has done... so the next generation would know them, even the children yet to be born, and they in turn would tell their children. Then they would put their trust in God and would not forget his deeds but would keep his commands. ...not like their forefathers – a stubborn and rebellious generation. (Psalm 78:3-8)

Everyone who quotes proverbs will quote this proverb about you: "Like mother, like daughter." You are a true daughter of your mother, who despised her husband and her children. You are a true sister of your sisters, who despised their husbands and their children. (Ezekiel 16:44-45)

No one has perfect parents. Even Christian parents, who care well for their children can and do fail in ways that damage their children. After all, they were not brought up in a perfect home either.

A common failure in fathers today is not taking responsibility for the spiritual well-being of their children. Sadly many fathers, even Christian ones, fail by leaving the instruction of children in the ways of God to mothers. This is not to belittle the place of mothers in nurturing, caring and teaching their children, but fathers have an important role in feeding God's truth into their children's spirit and to encourage and affirm them in their manliness and womanhood.

God calls husbands to love their wives as Christ loves the church and wives to honour and respect their husbands. (Ephesians 5:21-33) When children grow up in a family where this pattern has not been followed, boys can grow up absorbing an inner hatred of women and girls learn to despise men. When they marry they never intend these attitudes of hatred of women or despising of men to apply to their spouse, but what is hidden in the heart has the potential to harm the marriage. Recognition of such issues in our family is the first step towards their healing.

Completing the Family Tree

Here is a list of some things to consider about family background when completing a family tree.

Negative Emotions: anger, bitterness, pride, fear, grief, disappointment, suppressed emotions.

Rejection: through separation, divorce, adoption, death, over-protection, perfectionism, neglect, abuse (emotional, physical or sexual).

Family Failures: fathers who fail to lead spiritually, mothers who dominate, excessive punishment, over-protection, possessiveness, neglect, etc.

Social and Relationship Problems: alcohol or drug abuse, other addictions, domination, hatred of women, despising of men.

Sexual Sins: adultery, sex before marriage, sexual abuse, perversions.

Untimely Death: miscarriage, termination of pregnancy, traumatic or accidental death, suicide, war death.

Curses and Pronouncements: negative or binding words spoken into the family.

Cultural and Religious Influences: religious restriction and oppression, denominational control, legalism, aggressive nationalism, political extremism, racialism, curses, cults, occult involvement, freemasonry, martial arts, eastern religions, new age etc.

Illnesses and Weaknesses: hereditary illnesses, recurrent sicknesses, mental instability in the family etc.

Figure 2 is a fictitious family tree, in the process of being built up. When a family tree chart is complete it could look very complicated but it will provide a good guide when beginning to pray for the person.

OUTLINE FOR FAMILY TREE

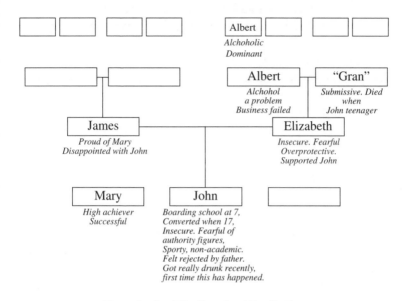

Figure 2. Partially Completed Family Tree

Example prayers

Examples of prayers are given below for use as a guide and outline. Always remember that it is a privilege to pray for others and involves their trust. It is best if you have a prayer partner to join you so that two can share the praying when you pray for other people's healing. Never push them to tell you more than they feel they can. You do not need to know all the details. God knows all about them anyway and He is the one who is the healer. So when people unfold their story to you it is important to assure them that what they say will be held in complete confidence. After prayer has been completed, the family tree, or any other notes made can be given to the person to keep themselves. What has been shared in the privacy of a place of prayer must never be shared without the explicit permission of the person concerned.

The following prayers are examples of the kind of prayers that can be used. Lead the person by praying through them slowly. It may help to give the person with whom you are praying a copy of the prayers to use, but it is usually better to lead them phrase by phrase, so that you can add to the prayers where necessary. Take time to work through and recall things that have come to light in compiling the family tree. It may also be helpful to pray through one side of the family first, dealing with issues on the father's side, say, and then returning to the mother's side, perhaps after a break. Respect the person you are praying with and do not attempt to do too much. Where deep emotions are involved give time for their expression. If there is a demonic manifestation, bind it in the name of Jesus, to stop any interference in the praying. It can be cast out later. It is not necessary to deal with everything all at once. Stop the prayer when the person has had enough and continue another day.

At the beginning of a prayer session it is good for the person concerned to acknowledge the Lordship of Jesus and to welcome the Holy Spirit's work in their lives as they choose to cooperate with Him. Pray for God's protection on all involved. Remembering the commandment *"Honour your father and your mother"*, it is also good to ask the person to begin by thanking God for parents, through whom life came and for every blessing received through the family line. Then go on to the confession of sins in the family background.

Confession of Generational Sin

Father God, I come to you in the name of Jesus Christ my Saviour and Lord. I confess that I and my ancestors have sinned and done evil in your sight.

Thank you, Father, for sending your only Son, Jesus, to die in my place; to pay the penalty for my sins through His shed blood and to bear the consequences for the iniquities of my ancestors when His body was bruised and pierced on the Cross.

I choose now, to confess, acknowledge and turn away from the sins of my parents and forebears back to the fourth generation and to the tenth generation for sexual sins. I acknowledge that they were sinners like I am. I specifically confess and acknowledge the sins and iniquities, hurts and illnesses of

38

.... (here mention any known sins, weaknesses etc. that have come to light in drawing up the family tree). *I bring before you all other iniquities in my family that have affected me adversely and I turn from them.*

Thank you, Father, that Jesus is my Holy Scapegoat and that He can set me free from the effects of the iniquities in my family. Thank you, too, Father, that He was wounded that I may be healed and that He carried all my griefs and sorrows. I now bring all these iniquities and sorrows to You. Thank you Father that You have laid them on the bruised and broken body of Jesus on the cross. I ask this prayer in the name of Jesus, my Saviour and my Lord. Amen.

Personal Confession and Repentance

Father, I confess that I too am a sinner and that I have sinned in some of the same ways as my ancestors. I now confess and repent of these sins which I have committed .... I also confess that my response to those who have sinned against me has not always been godly. I confess that I have been .... (angry, resentful, hateful, bitter, fearful, etc.) *I am sorry for this and repent of such behaviour and ask you to forgive me and cleanse me; in the Name of Jesus. Amen.*

Forgiveness of Ancestors

Father God, before You, I choose to forgive my forebears for all the things they have done which have affected me badly. I forgive .... (name the family member concerned and the specific sins, curses, pronouncements etc. involved and also declare a general forgiveness to other ancestors). *I renounce the consequences of these sins in my life, as well as the consequences of other sins unknown to me but known to You back to the fourth generation in my family and to the tenth generation for sexual sins. I take hold of and apply the truth that Jesus bore these iniquities as my Scapegoat, when they were laid on His bruised and broken body on the cross. Thank you that through Him I no longer have to carry these burdens. I release my ancestors into the freedom of my forgiveness. No longer will I blame them for how I am. Thank you Jesus for bearing away these iniquities so that I can be free. Amen.*

Breaking Ungodly Soul-Ties

This prayer is best prayed on behalf of the person you are praying with. Remember that the work of Christ on the cross is the only authority by which an ungodly tie can be broken.

In the name of the Father, the Son and the Holy Spirit, I break the ungodly soul-tie between you and .... (name the other person) I sever the ungodly linking in spirit, soul and body and place the cross of Christ between you and (the person). Together we take hold of the truth that the consequence of this iniquity has been borne by Jesus. It stops at the Cross which now separates you from (the other person). Thank you Father, in the name of Jesus. Amen.

Often there will be an expression of emotion at this point or perhaps earlier, when prayers for forgiveness or repentance have been prayed. Be ready to allow those you pray with to express their emotions as they surface. If necessary go on to pray for emotional or physical healing at this point or possibly to pray for deliverance and cleansing from any evil or unclean spirit that may have found a foothold in the person through ties in the family line. As you finish praying ask God to send His Holy and Life-giving Spirit to bless, protect and fill the person. Pray that God will continue the healing work which has begun and bring it to completion.

Cautions when Praying

If you are not already used to praying for the healing of people's emotional or physical hurts or for deliverance if they need it, you will need to seek further help and instruction. Full treatment of these subjects is not within the scope of this book.

As you hear about a person's family background and listen to their story you may begin to suspect or guess at things that may have happened. Also, you may receive a word of knowledge from the Holy Spirit giving you some revelation as a guide. Be very careful here and ask God for wisdom as you proceed. Satan is all too ready to use fertile imaginations and lead us down blind alleys. Great damage has been done by suggesting to people that they were abused as a child, or that they were involved in some satanic ritual. Never put such things on a person. People can have forgotten memories, but it is never wise to suggest to people what they might have forgotten. Always look for other independent evidence to corroborate any suspicions you may have. It is the truth that sets people free.

We are warned in 1 Timothy 1:4 not to devote ourselves to myths and endless genealogies. So avoid delving further and further back into the family history. We have the Bible's authority for looking back three or four generations (perhaps further for sexual sins). If we go beyond this we can again easily be led astray by Satan's lies. Even when we know that the origin of a family problem goes back many generations, dealing with the iniquities of three to four generations and breaking ungodly ties with parents will be sufficient.

Be ready to correct and lead people if necessary. For example when people are encouraged to pray forgiving their forebears some will begin: "O God, please forgive my father for…" If this happens gently interrupt them and ask them to start again. Point out that the purpose of this prayer is for them to express their own forgiveness to their ancestors, not to intercede on their behalf by asking God to forgive them. If they wish to go on to pray for God's mercy on any living relatives, encourage them to do so afterwards.

What about our own children?

We have often been asked "Is there anything we can do to prevent generational sin affecting our own children?" There is indeed

41

much that you can do. First you can apply the principles outlined in this book to yourself, dealing with the effects of the iniquity of past generations in your own life. Where your children are still young and dependent on you, they can be included in your prayers and you can break any ungodly strands in the ties that bond you with them. However if your children have grown to the age where they have begun to make important decisions for themselves or if they are adults, they will probably need prayer themselves. Perhaps the most important thing you can do when you realise that your children have been affected by your own sin, is to repent sincerely of that sin. You can also look for the opportunity to tell your children that you are sorry for things you did which harmed them. Above all you need to examine how you are still behaving towards them, even when they are grown up. As you do this, and continually pray for them, you will find that relationships grow better, and your children will not be as affected by the iniquity of past generations to the same extent as perhaps you were. If you are still concerned that their lives are affected, encourage them to ask the Lord to remove that iniquity by following the steps described in this book.

The Joy of Freedom and Healing

Dealing with iniquity from past generations is not always the main issue in the life of those who seek healing for physical, emotional or spiritual damage, but we have found that often it has been one of the main keys to bringing people to wholeness. We have witnessed many men and women receiving healing and emotional wholeness by accepting all that Jesus has done for them in dealing with generational iniquity. Often healing has come simply as people hear and appropriate to themselves the fullness of Jesus' work on the cross.

We have seen many being freed to make relationships in ways they were totally unable to previously; marriages being restored; parents and children being reconciled; addictions conquered; physical pains disappearing; compulsive behaviour stopped.

Bill, whose story we began with, was warned by his doctors

that there was a weakness in his leg and that the problem may recur, but he has been free of pain for six years and he has had the joy of being able to play games with his children. He had almost had to give up his job, which was a great worry to him, but he is still working and enjoying it.

It was a joy when Julia gave me a hug after she had been set free from the effects of sexual sin in her family, more than one generation back. It was a greater joy to see her hugging her father for the first time a few days later.

Another young man who was plagued with unfounded and irrational fears of having a heart attack was able to deal with the roots which had been in his grandfather. This freed him to continue his education which the fears had disrupted.

A lady lost her deep fear of people in authority when ungodly ties of domination from an autocratic great-grandfather which had affected her as a little girl were broken.

One woman's father had been reported killed in the first world war and her mother had suffered great grief. Then it was discovered that it was an error of mistaken identity and he was in fact recovering from wounds. Confusion and grief affected the family adversely. Many years later cancer developed in the lady and following operations and therapy she was nearly dying. When the generational grief and confusion were dealt with she made a remarkable recovery and enjoyed several more years of life in good health.

A man had a compulsion to stalk women which he had struggled to overcome for years and failed time and again. After dealing with the consequences of sexual sin in earlier generations the compulsion went and his marriage was saved.

Another man admitted that he and his family were restricted by a deeply held commitment to their clan motto, which was "Forget not". This acted as a restricting curse on his behaviour. After breaking ungodly ties with previous generations he was released from this curse and his will was freed to make right choices.

There is much more to each of these brief accounts and many other examples could be cited of people who have been healed physically, emotionally or in their relationships when issues from their family background have been dealt with using the principles described in this book. Jesus encouraged His disciples to carry on His work when He said: *I tell you the truth, anyone who has faith in me will do what I have been doing. He will do even greater things than these, because I am going to the Father.* (John 14:12) Praise God that the Saviour's work can continue as we do it in His name. Part of this is the wonderful work of repairing the devastation of generations.

> *The Spirit of the Sovereign Lord is on me, because the Lord has anointed me to preach good news to the poor.* **He has sent me to bind up the brokenhearted, to proclaim freedom for the captives and release from darkness for the prisoners,** *to proclaim the year of the Lord's favour and the day of vengeance of our God, to comfort all who mourn, and provide for those who grieve in Zion – to bestow on them a crown of beauty instead of ashes, the oil of gladness instead of mourning, and a garment of praise instead of a spirit of despair. They will be called oaks of righteousness, a planting of the Lord for the display of his splendour. They will rebuild the ancient ruins and restore the places long devastated; they will* **renew the ruined cities that have been devastated for generations.** (Isaiah 61:1-4)

Other titles available in the 'What Christians Should Know About....' series:

Depression Anxiety, Mood Swings and Hyperactivity
By Dr. Grant Mullen

The Endtime Harvest
By David Shibley

Escaping From Debt
By Keith Tondeur

Generational Sin
By Pennant Jones

The Glory of God
By Ed Roebert

How to Pray Effectiveley for Your Lost Loved Ones
By David Alsobrook

The Importance of Forgiveness
By John Arnott

A Personal Relationship with God
By Peter Nodding

Preparing for Christ's Return
By Clive Corfield

Reconciliation
By John Dawson

Sickness and Healing
By Ed Harding

Their Value to God
By Steve and Chris Hepden

Power Filled Worship
By Russ Hughes

If you have enjoyed this book and would like to help us to send a copy of it and many other titles to needy pastors in the **Third World**, please write for further information or send your gift to:

Sovereign World Trust, P.O. Box 777, Tonbridge, Kent TN11 0ZS, United Kingdom

or to the **'Sovereign World'** distributor in your country.